ANSWERING
ISLAM
WITH QUESTIONS

BY PHILIP DELRE

Voice Publishing USA

ANSWERING ISLAM WITH QUESTIONS

Philip DelRe

© Copyright 2009 by Voice Publishing

USA

Scripture taken from the New American Standard Bible. Used by permission.

ISBN 0-9677520-4-3

Printed in the United States of America.

CONTENTS

PREFACE

YOU NEED TO KNOW

Just as there are many Christians who are "Christian" in name only, there are many Muslims who are "Muslim" in name only. That is to say, they call themselves "Muslims," but they are not seriously committed to following the teachings of Islam, they do not study the Koran, and they are unaware of the origin of Islam, and are biblically illiterate. For these people, their religion is cultural rather than spiritual. Then you have the radical, fanatical (faithful) variety. Experts believe this group is growing and currently makes up about 20% of the total Muslim population.

In most Islamic nations, Saudi Arabia being a prime example, a great deal of pressure is exerted on people to follow Islam. This comes not only from the Islamic community, but also from family and "friends." Then they have the pressure of Islamic law and the religious police. Islamic (Sharia) law calls for the death of those who would reject or leave Islam, even if they are members of your own family. Obviously, under these circumstances it is very difficult to reach Muslims. Islam has spread over the last 1400 years in large part due to violence and from that has become known as "the religion of the sword." By contrast, Jesus Christ never forced anyone to do anything. His teaching was based on love. Forced love is a contradiction in terms. In John 14:15 Jesus said:

If you love Me, you will keep My commandments.

In this context, many Muslims may be quick to point out that the Crusades were carried out by "Christians," but that is *not* correct. The Crusaders were *Catholics*, authorized by Pope Urban II in the 11th century to fight back against Muslim aggression. Jerusalem had been taken by force from Christians and Jews in the 7th century. For political reasons, the Pope wanted to take Jerusalem for Rome! There is no way to justify murdering people for political reasons, personal gain, or because they don't want your religion—or any religion!

The Crusades lasted 300 years. By comparison, Islam holds the record for the longest killing streak in history—1,400 years and counting! Islam also holds the all-time record for the greatest number of murders. Ready for this? Since the seventh century, Islamic fundamentalists have murdered an estimated 270 million people, and that number is now growing exponentially. Islam has produced more carnage than WWI, WWII, Hitler, Stalin, and Mao Tse-tung combined! These numbers, and the numbers on almost every major war in history, can be verified at: *MarkHumphrys.com*. Mark has recorded these statistics based on real historical data. (He is an unbiased atheist; he hates all religions equally.)

Our goal in presenting this material is not to teach you how to win an argument, but how to win a soul. We choose to present this material in booklet form since most people will not read a 300 to 400 page, theologically technical book on Islam. So, we made this a quick, easy-to-use resource.

Much like the Jehovah's Witnesses, the typical Muslim's approach to proselytizing Christians in the United States is to point out a dozen or so alleged Bible difficulties or "contradictions." The false assumption is (since they claim the Bible contains errors), that Islam must be the correct and only alternative.

The fact of the matter is, to all objective seekers of truth, each of the alleged "errors" in the Bible has a good explanation. Secondly, as you are about to discover, the following statements taken directly from the Koran and the Hadith (the so-called sayings of Mohammed) make the so called "Bible difficulties" seem utterly insignificant by comparison!

Since the Muslim claims the Bible is in error, and the Koran is perfect, the burden of proof clearly lies with him or her to explain the bizarre and erroneous statements found in the Koran and the Hadith *before* attempting to disprove the Bible. These statements are documented in the pages to follow.

TEN FAST TRACK QUESTIONS FOR MUSLIMS

ASK... a Muslim any of the following questions. If he answers "no" to any of them, according to Islamic law he must die as an infidel.

1. Do you believe the sun sets in a puddle of mud? (See pg. 43)

2. Do you believe that Adam was nine stories tall? (See pg. 43)

3. Would you agree with Mohammed if he said that non-Muslims have seven intestines, and Muslims have only one? (See pg. 43)

4. Why, if a Muslim prays while looking up, his eyes will be snatched away? (See pg. 44)

5. Mohammed said, "A fly has a disease on one wing and the cure for that disease on the other." How do you account for that? (See pg. 45)

6. The Koran says Mohammed performed no miracles, but the Hadith says he did. Which one is wrong? (See pg. 47)

7. How can Satan urinate in the ear of a Muslim if he sleeps during prayer time since he is a non-material being? (See pg. 50)

8. How can Satan spend the night in your nose if you become ceremonially unclean? Do you believe that? (See pg. 50)

9. What qualifies Mohammed as a prophet? (See pg. 52)

10. If Islam is true, why does the Koran say you may lose your faith if you examine the evidence? (See pg. 46)

CHAPTER ONE

THE LAW OF NON-CONTRADICTION— AN INSURMOUNTABLE PROBLEM FOR ISLAM

In logic, the law of non-contradiction states that two antithetical propositions cannot both be true and false at the same time and in the same sense. Philip Johnson explains it this way,

> . . . nothing that is true can be self-contradictory or inconsistent with any other truth. All logic depends on this simple principle. Rational thought and meaningful discourse demand it. To deny it is to deny all truth in one fell swoop. Until a little more than a hundred years ago, the law of contradiction was almost universally accepted by philosophers as a self-evident truth. Francis Schaeffer attributed the decline of 20th-century society to the demise of the law of contradiction. Scripture very clearly affirms the law of non-contradiction. First John 2:21, for example is explicit: "No lie is of the truth." Many other passages, such as 2 Timothy 2:13, "God cannot deny himself" either assume or reiterate the law of non-contradiction.

So what does all this have to do with Islam? Everything—keep reading!

The Koran says that Moses, Jesus, and Mohammed were true prophets of God. It also states that the Bible, both the Old and the New Testaments, were revealed by Allah. *The Koran states explicitly that Allah's word cannot be changed, altered, or corrupted.*

According to Islam, the Koran completes the Old and the New Testament, and Allah is the author of all three.

In Sura 29:46, the Koran, referring to "the people of the book" (Jews and Christians) says: "Our God and your God are one." That is impossible, and creates an insurmountable problem for Islam since the Koran and the Bible contradict each other on virtually every major point of theology.

MUTUAL EXCLUSIVITY

If we can demonstrate irreconcilable contradictions on virtually every major doctrine between Christianity and Islam, then we are forced to the inescapable conclusion that either, the Bible *and* the Koran are false, or one is true and the other is false. They *cannot* both be correct and, therefore, could not have been written by the same author as Islam claims.

Muslims are taught that the Bible has been corrupted and the Koran has not. Yet, there are more than 100 references to the Old and the New Testaments in the Koran. Showing a Muslim what the Koran itself says about the Bible will either stop his mouth or cause him to contradict the Koran.

ASK...

- *How do you explain the following verses in the Koran?*

"We (Allah) gave Moses the Book and followed him up with a succession of messengers" (Sura 2:87).

"We (Allah) have sent thee inspiration, as We sent it to Noah and the Messengers after him: we sent inspiration to Abraham, Isma'il, Isaac, Jacob and the Tribes, to Jesus, Job, Jonah, Aaron, and Solomon, and to David We gave the Psalms" (Sura 4:163).

"It is He (Allah) Who sent down to thee (step by step), in truth, the Book, confirming what went before it; and He sent down the Law (of Moses) and the Gospel (of Jesus) before this, as a guide to mankind, and He sent down the criterion (of judgment between right and wrong)" (Sura 3:3).

"And in their footsteps We sent Jesus the son of Mary, confirming the Law that had come before him: We sent him the Gospel: therein was guidance and light, and confirmation of the Law that had come before him: a guidance and an admonition to those who fear Allah" (Sura 5:46).

"Rejected were the messengers before thee: with patience and constancy they bore their rejection and their wrongs, until Our aid did reach them: there is none that can alter the words (and decrees) of Allah. Already hast thou received some account of those messengers" (Sura 6:34).

"The word of thy Lord doth find its fulfillment in truth and in justice: None can change His words: for He is the one who heareth and knoweth all" (Sura 6:115).

"This Koran could not have been composed by any except Allah; but it is a confirmation of that which was revealed before it, and an explanation of the scripture; there is no doubt thereof, sent down from the Lord of all creatures" (Sura 10:37).

"For them are glad tidings, in the life of the present and in the hereafter; no change can there be in the words of Allah. This is indeed the supreme felicity" (Sura 10:64).

ASK...

- *Why do you not believe the Koran when it says the Bible is the Word of Allah and cannot be altered, changed, or corrupted?*

- *On what authority do you overrule Mohammed and the Koran?*

The Koran says the Bible was written by Allah and cannot be changed; that leaves only three possibilities:

1. Either Allah is not all-powerful and therefore unable to protect his word,

2. Or Mohammad was wrong and the Koran has an error, or,

3. The Koran is correct and the Bible has *not* been corrupted. Which is it?

TEN IRRECONCILABLE CONTRADICTIONS PROVE THE KORAN AND THE BIBLE COULD NOT HAVE BEEN WRITTEN BY THE SAME AUTHOR

1. The Nature Of God

The God of the Bible is sovereign, yet personal, and knowable. He is intimately involved in the affairs of the world and of men. He personally appeared in a cloud and spoke audibly to the entire nation of Israel on Mt. Sinai in Exodus 20. He spoke through angels, prophets, and apostles. He spoke through visions and dreams, signs and wonders. He can even speak through a donkey if He wants to!

God's complete plan of redemption is realized through the written and the Living Word of God—the Bible and Jesus Christ. According to Exodus 3:15, His most holy and proper name to *all* generations is YHWH. The name "Allah" never appears even once in the Bible. Jesus said, when we pray, we can call God "Our Father!" He seeks a personal love relationship with His people.

The Bible also teaches the triune nature of God —Father, Son and Holy Spirit. For proof of the Trinity, see page 57. According to Sura 5:73, the doctrine of the Trinity is blasphemy, but in 5:116, whoever wrote the Koran mistakenly thought that the Trinity consisted of God, Jesus, and Mary! That was never the Biblical position.

By contrast, the God of Islam completely transcends his creation and is unknowable. Islam teaches that God's most holy and proper name is Allah—not YHWH. The relationship between Allah and

Muslims is based on reverence and fear, not love. There are 99 names for God in Islam, and Father is *not* one of them.

The idea of having a personal love relationship with Allah is a foreign concept to Muslims.

2. The Nature Of Jesus Christ

According to the New Testament, believing in the deity of Jesus Christ is absolutely essential to salvation. In John 8:26 Jesus said, "... you shall die in your sins; for unless you believe that I am (*He*) you shall die in your sins." John 1:1 and Colossians 1:17 state that Jesus was God manifested in human flesh, eternal and not created.

Anyone can say they he or she is a prophet, anyone can *say* I am God—proving it is much more difficult. There are seven "I am" sayings of Jesus in the New Testament. Each one is a clear reference to Exodus 3:14 when God revealed one of His names to Moses: "I am, that I am, tell them I am." So, when Jesus said, "Before Abraham was I am," the Pharisees knew *exactly* what He meant, and they proved this by wanting to stone Him for claiming to be God (John 8:58, 59; 10:30,31)!

Jesus said, "I am the light of the world." But, He did not just *say,* "I am the light of the world," He *said,* "I am the light of the world," as He gave sight to a man born blind! He did not just *say,* "I am the bread of life." He *said,* "I am the bread of life," and He fed five thousand people! He did not just *say,* "I am the resurrection and the life." He *said,* "I am the resurrection and the life," as He called forth Lazarus from the dead! Each of the "I am" sayings was accompanied by a miracle, which in turn revealed attributes that belong to God alone. For example, the one miracle that Jesus performed more than any other was giving sight to the blind. Compare that to what God said to Moses in Exodus 4:11:

And the LORD said to him, "Who has made man's mouth? Or who makes him dumb or deaf, or seeing or blind? Is it not I, the LORD?"

These three "I am" examples show that Jesus not only claimed to be God, but offered empirical proof of being the Creator, the Sustainer, and the Redeemer of all mankind. He proved His verbal claims with literal miracles.

Jesus said, "Peace, be still," and the winds and the sea obeyed Him. He said, "Destroy this temple, and in three days I will raise it." He was speaking of raising Himself bodily from the dead. Only God can do that! In Matt. 9:2, Jesus said to the paralytic, "Your sins are forgiven." Who can forgive sin but God alone? No man ever spoke like Jesus before or since. See also Jn. 1:1-2, 14; 8:24; 10:30; 14:9; 20:24-28, Lk. 5:19-21, Col. 1:15-17, Titus 2:13, Rev. 22:13-16.)

And finally, in I John 2:22 the Bible says, "Who is the liar but the one who denies that Jesus is the Christ? This is the antichrist, the one who denies the Father and the Son."

That is exactly what Islam has done. Both in the Koran and etched in stone on the Mosque of Omar, it says, "God forbid that Allah should have a son." In Islam, the idea of God having a son is an abomination and considered a gross blasphemy. It is a sin on a par with rape, murder, incest, and child abuse. The Koran says the fires of Hell await those who believe that Jesus Christ is the Son of God. Indeed, according to John 8:24, Jesus Himself said that believing in His deity was essential to salvation! Therefore, the author of the Bible cannot be the author of the Koran. According to the Mohammed, Allah created Jesus from dust just as Adam was created.

Mohammed said Jesus was a true prophet, but Jesus said He was truly God. Jesus backed His claim by doing things only God can do. If Jesus was not God, then He was either a liar or a lunatic. Yet Mohammed said Jesus was a prophet without sin! "If Jesus was right, Mohammed was wrong, and if Jesus was wrong, Mohammed was still wrong because Mohammed said Jesus was right!"

3. The Nature Of Man

The Bible teaches that when Adam sinned, his body was cursed, and all of his descendants inherited the sin nature. All men are sinners by nature and by choice. All men sin and that is why all men die.

Islam teaches that man is born without sin, is basically good, and *may* be forgive him on judgment day if his good works outweigh his bad works.

4. The Bible

The Bible claims to be perfect, complete, and literally "God breathed" (2 Tim 3:16). It reveals God's perfect and complete plan for the redemption of mankind. Unlike any other book in history, it was written over the course of 1500 years, on three continents, in three languages, by 40 different writers from every walk of life (from kings to fishermen). The Bible answers the most profound questions beating in the human heart, namely: Who am I; Where did I come from? Where am I going when I die? If God is good, why is there evil? How can I be free from the guilt and the power of sin? How did the world begin, how it will end, and how do I get to heaven?

The story of the Bible unfolds in and through history. Contrary to popular opinion, the Bible does not start out "Once upon a time." The story of the New Testament begins, "In Bethlehem, of Judea, in the time of King Herod." Hundreds of names, dates, times, places, and events are recorded in great detail. It speaks on hundreds of controversial topics, yet it has a beginning, a middle, and an end, even though the first and last writers were separated by a span of 1,500 years!

The Bible states unequivocally that the ultimate proof of its divine authenticity is found within its own pages through predictive prophecy. Why? Because only someone with the attribute of omniscience can tell us what will happen in the future with 100% accuracy. In Isaiah chapters 40-44, God challenges all other gods and/or religions to do the same. According to Scripture, prophecy was given so that the nations may know that He (God) is the LORD, and there is no other (Ezek. 36:23).

Islam teaches that the Bible is incomplete and has been corrupted. Muslims believe the Koran is the final and complete revelation of Allah. The ultimate proof that the Koran is divinely inspired, according to Islam, is based on the eloquence of its literature. The Koran itself challenges the world to produce even a single paragraph from any book in history that is more beautiful than any single paragraph found in the Koran. Using this logic, then one might say, if a Ferrari is the most beautiful car in the world, it must have been manufactured by God, or that a woman's beauty is proof of her virtue. Eloquence, real or perceived, is *not* empirical proof of divinity. Apart from the Bible, Shakespeare is believed by many to be the most eloquent literature in English. Would that be proof that God wrote it?

Appendix One of this booklet deals in much greater detail with the challenge to compare any chapter in the Koran to any other literature. This is a must read for who want to know the truth about Islam's claim that the Koran is divine because of its peerless literature.

5. Sin And Salvation

In 1 John 3:4, the Bible says that "sin is the transgression of the law." From Romans 3:23 and 6:23 we know that all men have sinned, and that is why all men die. All the good works in the world cannot reverse the effect of sin, which is death. God's decree to Adam and Eve was, "If you sin you shall surely die." God is perfectly holy, righteous, just, and true. As such, He cannot allow even one sin to go unpunished, or He Himself would be unjust.

HOW DO YOU RECONCILE JUSTICE AND MERCY WITHOUT COMPROMISING JUSTICE?

That is the whole point of the Bible. Since the penalty for sin is death, and since all men have sinned, in order for a Savior to save you He would have to be sinless and die for you. That is what Jesus, the sinless Lamb of God, did on the cross. That is why the Bible teaches that we are saved by grace alone, through faith alone, through Christ alone, plus—nothing! Our good works are the result of our salvation, never the cause of it.

Islam teaches that man is not born a sinner and is basically good. Two angels keep track of all your good deeds and all your bad deeds. If your good deeds out-weigh your bad deeds, Allah *may* have mercy on you. There is one exception. If you murder or dis-member an infidel (Jews and Christians are specifically named), then you are guaranteed a place in Paradise. For men, heaven is a place of wine and women. The Muslim men are promised unlimited sex with 70 perpetual virgins, and wine. This is ironic in light of the fact that adultery and alcohol are forbidden as sin in this life! (No one knows what the women receive.)

6. The Ten Commandments

The Bible teaches that the Ten Commandments were given directly by God Himself, written by His own "finger" on tablets of stone, and on the heart of every man (Rom. 2:15). The importance of the Ten Commandments in biblical theology cannot be overstated. Understanding the nature of sin is a non-optional prerequisite for understanding the need for salvation. According to Exodus 20:20, Romans 7:7, and 1 John 1:9, the Ten Commandments define what sin is, and God's definition of sin has never changed. Between the Koran and the Hadith, Islam has literally reversed each and every one of the Ten Commandments (see Chapter Two).

7. Jews and Christians

According to the Bible, Jews and Christians (by way of prophets and apostles) were the very people entrusted and inspired by God to write the scriptures—God's message of salvation—to the world. The Jews were God's "chosen people" for this mission.

In the Koran, Jews and Christians are specifically targeted as "infidels" and must die if they refuse to accept the teachings of Islam.

8. God's Plan For Israel

The Bible clearly states in Genesis 17:8, and in dozens of other verses, that God gave the land of Israel to the Jews. In the Old Testament, God identifies Himself as the God of Abraham, Isaac, and Jacob, and as the God of Israel hundreds of times! God gave the land to Abraham and his descendants as part of an everlasting covenant, which was recorded 4,000 years ago, beginning in Genesis chapter 12. According to the Bible (which was completed 600 years before Mohammed was even born), the land of Israel is the key to God's prophetic time-clock, His revelation of Himself to the world, and His plan of redemption. John 4:22 says, "Salvation is of the Jews." The Bible was written in Israel by Israelis (with the exception of Luke and Acts which were written by Luke, who was a Gentile). Jesus, came to earth as a Jew, He shed His blood on Israeli soil, and offered His life as a sacrifice for the sin of the world.

ISRAEL IS GOD'S PROPHETIC TIME-CLOCK

Much of biblical prophecy is centered in and around Israel's past, present, and future. Since only God can predict the future with 100% accuracy, God pre-wrote Israel's history in stunning detail, hundreds and even thousands of years in advance so the nations may KNOW that He is God and there is no other!

In Isaiah 40-44 God says,

I am the first and I am the last. There is no God besides Me. Only I can declare the end from the beginning.

In essence, God is saying, "If you think you've got a god, okay, let him (or her) step up to the plate and predict the future! Why? Because only the True and Living God can do that!

One of the most spectacular passages of biblical prophecy concerns Israel and is found in Ezek. 36-39. Written 2500 years ago, Ezekiel prophesied that the entire nation of Israel would be exiled because of its sin. Furthermore, the land would remain desolate for a long time, and in the "latter days" God would bring His people back and exalt them once again as a nation.

The Jewish nation began some 4,000 years ago with one man — Abraham. Abraham had Isaac, Isaac had Jacob. Jacob had twelve sons who became the twelve tribes of the nation of Israel. The next scene introduces Joseph, who saves the family from starvation in Egypt. After 400 years in Egypt, the original family of 70 became a nation of 2-3 million people. Moses brings them out of Egypt to Mt. Sinai where God gives them their Constitution and their Declaration of Independence — the Ten Commandments. Move the clock ahead 1,500 years, and the Roman Empire is ruling the world with an iron fist when Jesus comes on the scene. In Matthew 24, Jesus tells us what will happen to Israel and her people—the nation will fall by the sword, the city of Jerusalem and the Temple will be destroyed, and the Jews will be scattered to the ends of the earth.

In A.D. 70, almost forty years after Jesus ascended to Heaven, General Titus and the Roman army destroyed Jerusalem, and the Jews were exiled to the four corners of the earth. Miraculously, they remained a distinct race of people even though they had no homeland for almost 2,000 years! Then, in 1939, World War II began. One of Hitler's goals was to exterminate the Jews, as the final solution to Germany's problems. When Hitler was finally stopped in 1945, 6,000,000 Jews had been murdered. After the war, the surviving Jews began to trickle back into their ancient homeland. Then, in 1948, they established a second Jewish state. Bull's eye—precisely as the Bible predicted thousands of years earlier. Never before in the history of geopolitics have we seen anything that even begins to compare to biblical prophecy and the nation of Israel.

Since its re-establishment in 1948, Israel has been in a constant state of war. Israel has suffered five full-blown attacks by its Arab neighbors, and though vastly out-numbered each time, God gave overwhelming victories to Israel, and each time, her borders have expanded. This is a deep embarrassment to Islam. Israel is one of the smallest nations on earth (there are only five million Jews living there), and they are surrounded by 350 million Arabs—yet, the Jews cannot be defeated militarily. Why? Because in Jeremiah 31:35-37, God said that you would have a better chance of changing the course of the sun, the moon and the stars than removing the Jews from Israel ever again! Their scientific discoveries, their technology, their GDP, their agriculture, their military capabilities, the disproportionate number of Nobel prizes they have won, and their standard of living represent some of the greatest achievements in world history.

The Middle East Crisis In A Nutshell

According to the Bible, God promised the land to Abraham, to his "son of promise," Isaac, and to their descendants. More than 2,600 years later, Mohammed claimed that Ishmael (not Isaac) was the rightful heir, and therefore the land belongs to the Arabs. That is why radical (faithful) Muslims are so determined to destroy Israel and take the land. If Israel prevails (or even exists), Muslims will be forced to admit that Allah is not the true God, Mohammed was not a prophet, and the Koran is false! *That is the crux of the Middle East conflict.*

Ultimately, the battle is not between Jews and Arabs; God loves them both. The battle is between the forces of darkness and the Prince of Peace. If Satan can annihilate the Jews, and destroy the state of Israel, the biblical prophecy that Jesus will return to rule from David's throne in Jerusalem cannot be fulfilled. That is why Satan must destroy Israel. The Bible says that Antichrist will seat himself in the Temple and claim to be God!

In Zechariah 14:1-4 and Joel 3, the Bible clearly states that the last war of the world will be fought over Jerusalem (more proof that the Bible is true). Incredibly, the voice of prophecy says that the LORD Himself will fight the nations that come against Israel, He will defeat them and Jesus will return to rule on David's throne forever! Islam teaches that the Jews of Israel must be wiped off the map because they have taken the land that rightfully belongs to Muslims. Jews are referred to as "dogs and pigs." Islam teaches that Ishmael, not Isaac, was Abraham's rightful heir. Therefore, Islam must be vindicated and the entire Jewish race must be annihilated before the world will know "peace."

9. Jesus Dying On The Cross

The Bible explicitly states that the disciples were eyewitnesses of the death, burial, and resurrection of Jesus Christ. But, why did Jesus have to die? The answer is found in the Old Testament. The sacrificial system was ordained by God. It provided the world with 1,500 years of literal, historical, and theological context so that when Jesus offered Himself as a perfect sacrifice for sin, it would all make sense. Remember what John the Baptist said when he saw Jesus? "Behold the *Lamb of God* who takes away the sin of the world." John understood—the only way God could reconcile justice and mercy without compromising His justice was through the death of a sinless sacrifice. You cannot approach the throne of God without a blood sacrifice and live to tell about it.

Since the penalty for sin is death, in order for a savior to save you, he would have to be sinless and die for you. This makes perfect sense.

Jesus Christ is the central theme of the Bible from Genesis to Revelation. Unlike the founders of other religions, if you take Christ out of Christianity, you have nothing.

In Sura 4:157, the Koran says that Jesus did *not* die on the cross. Allah would never allow such an important prophet to be crucified; Jesus was translated into heaven and never died. In the strictest sects of Islam, Muslim children are taught that the Christian God is an archaic, blood-thirsty vampire who enjoys human sacrifice and is a child abuser.

10. To Love Or To Hate Your Enemies?

Jesus taught his followers to love their enemies.

- Matthew 5:44: "But I say unto you, love your enemies, bless them that curse you, do good to them that hate you, and pray for them which despitefully use you, and persecute you."

- Matthew 6:14: "For if ye forgive men their trespasses, your heavenly Father will also forgive you: But if ye forgive not men their trespasses, neither will your Father forgive your trespasses."

Mohammed taught his followers to murder their enemies .

There are 123 verses in the Koran that call for murdering or dismembering anyone who refuses to submit to Islam (The Bible clearly states that unrepentant murderers will *not* inherit the kingdom of Heaven). Here are just a few examples:

- Sura 2:216: "Fighting is prescribed for you."

- Sura 4:104: "Seek out your enemies relentlessly."

- Sura 8:12: "I will cast terror into the hearts of those who disbelieve. Therefore strike off their heads and strike off every fingertip of them"

- Sura 8:15: "O ye who believe! When ye meet those who disbelieve in battle, turn not your backs to them. Whoso on that day turneth his back to them, unless maneuvering for battle or intent to join a company, he truly hath incurred wrath from Allah, and his habitation will be hell, a hapless journey's end."

- Sura 9:12: "...make war on the leaders of unbelief...Make war on them: God will chastise them at your hands and humble them. He will grant you victory over them..."

- Sura 9:27: "Fight against such as those to whom the Scriptures were given [Jews and Christians]...until they pay tribute out of hand and are utterly subdued."

- Sura 9:73: "Prophet make war on the unbelievers and the hypocrites and deal rigorously with them. Hell shall be their home."

CONCLUSION

This is just a sample of the dozens of contradictions that exist between Christianity and Islam. The Koran maintains that both the Bible and the Koran were inspired by the same author—Allah. And, since the Koran claims that Allah's word cannot be altered, corrupted, or changed, this presents an insurmountable problem for the Muslim.

RECONCILING JUSTICE AND MERCY

Now He [Jesus] said to them, "These are My words which I spoke to you while I was still with you, that all things which are written about Me in the Law of Moses and the Prophets and the Psalms must be fulfilled" Luke 24:44.

So the world would know the Bible is no man-made conspiracy, there are 1,500 years between the first and last writers of scripture (Moses and John). And, just to make doubly sure, there are 400 years of silence in between the last book of the Old Testament and the first book of the New Testament.

Incredibly, the Bible was written by 40 different authors from every walk of life. Moses was a prince who lived in the palace of Pharaoh, the King of Egypt. Amos was a herdsman; Joshua was a military general; Daniel was a prime minister; David was a king; Luke was a doctor; Paul was a rabbi; Peter was a fisherman; and Matthew was a tax collector!

The Bible was written on three continents: Asia, Africa, and Europe, and written in three languages: Hebrew, Aramaic, and Greek. Yet it is one book, with a beginning, middle and an end. It speaks on hundreds of controversial topics with perfect unity, even though the first and last writers were separated by a span of 1,500 years! The Paradise lost in the book of Genesis is regained in the book of Revelation. Jesus Christ, crowned with thorns in the Gospels, is crowned with glory in the New Jerusalem. There is only one possible explanation for the miraculous nature of the Bible—there were 40 writers, but only one author!

Furthermore, God divided the Bible in two Testaments. Without the New Testament, the Old Testament would be incomplete, and without the Old Testament, the New Testament would be utterly incomprehensible. Each is a guide to properly understanding the other. The Old Testament is the foundation upon which the New Testament is built, and the New Testament constantly refers back to the Old Testament to verify its authority. Through fulfilled prophecy, each points back and forth to the other as proof positive of its divine authenticity and its perfect unity.

The very first verse in the New Testament forces you to this inescapable conclusion. Matthew 1:1 shows us two things: first, that God always keeps His promises, and secondly, that the Bible is one book. See for yourself:

> This is the record of the genealogy of Jesus Christ the Son of David, the Son of Abraham.

This verse says in effect, "If you are starting here, you have to go back to Genesis, brother!" Who would pick up any other book and start reading right in the middle? Yet, people do that with the Bible, and wonder why they have trouble understanding it. Michael Horton put it this way, "Starting in Matthew is like walking into a movie half-way through. It's like thinking you are telling a good joke when all you can remember is the punch line!"

Without understanding the covenant promises that God made to Abraham and David, Matt. 1:1 would be utterly boring. But, when you understand them in light of the Old Testament promises of a Savior to come, this verse explodes with excitement! Matthew 1:1 says in effect, "The Messiah has come. Just as it was written!"

This same principle holds true for more than 1,200 verses in the New Testament. What is the significance of Christ dying on Passover and being raised on First Fruits were it not for the book of Exodus? What sense would John have made when he said of Jesus, "Behold the Lamb of God who takes away the sin of the world," or Jesus when He said, "This is the new covenant in My blood," were it not for the doctrine of the blood atonement established in the book of Leviticus?

The sacrificial system went on for 1500 years, providing us with a literal, historical, and theological context, so when Jesus died on the cross this would all make sense!

In the Old Testament sacrificial system, the priest would offer a lamb without spot or blemish. No lame or blind animals could be used. God is trying to tell us something—He can only accept a perfect sacrifice. The whole thing was a huge object lesson. The sacrificial system went on for 1,500 years! Why? To provide us with a literal, historical, and theological context, so when Jesus died on the cross it would all make sense.

This fascinating form of biblical prophecy is called "type" and "antitype". A type is a foreshadowing, a picture, a symbol, a precursor, an object lesson if you will, that typifies Christ and salvation. A type is an actual historical event in the Old Testament that typifies, portrays, or symbolizes a New Testament spiritual truth. The New Testament fulfillment is called the antitype. One of the best examples of a type and antitype is found in the book of Exodus. The Israelites were "redeemed" from 400 years of Egyptian slavery. This actual, historical event portrayed a much larger spiritual truth that finds its fulfillment in the New Testament.

Pharaoh typified Satan. He would not let God's people go. Slavery in Egypt represented slavery to sin. The Hebrews cried out to God for deliverance. That is how salvation begins—with prayer. In response, God instructed them to slaughter a lamb and paint the blood over their doorposts vertically and horizontally. This pictures the blood of the cross of Jesus Christ — the Lamb of God (see 1 Cor. 5:7-b). Then, the Angel of Death, seeing the blood, would "Passover" them, sparing them from God's judgment which was death! What happened next? Freed from slavery, they headed for the Promised Land with all the riches of Egypt.

This typifies the rich inheritance that awaits God's people in the promised land of heaven. This "salvation" was accomplished not by the good works of the Hebrew people, but by the hand of God.

EXAMPLE # 2

The story of Abraham and Isaac is another prime example of the Biblical type. God promised Abraham a son when, humanly speaking, that was impossible. Isaac is called "the son of promise" because he was born to a 100-year-old father and a 90-year-old mother who previously had borne no children. Isaacs's birth was a type of Christs' virgin birth. There was also a long period between the promise of a son and his actual birth. In exactly the same way, God promised a Savior back in Genesis. Then, after a 4,000 year long wait a child was born, miraculously to a virgin!

Then, in Genesis 22, we read of God's call to Abraham to sacrifice his son. Abraham had to walk three days to reach Mt. Moriah. So, for all practical purposes, Isaac was dead (in Abraham's mind) for three days! Christ, the sinless Lamb of God, was sacrificed exactly where Abraham took Isaac, on Mt. Moriah. Jesus, God's only begotten Son was dead for three days. Isaac was a type of Christ (see Heb. 11:17-19). Remember what Isaac asked Abraham just prior to the sacrifice on Mt. Moriah in Gen 22:7-8?

And Isaac spoke to Abraham his father and said, "My father!" And he said, "Here I am, my son." And he said, "Behold, the fire and the wood, but where is the lamb for the burnt offering?"

And Abraham said, "God will provide for Himself the lamb for the burnt offering, my son."

God did provide the sacrifice. He gave His only begotten Son. The whole thing pointed us to Jesus!

EXAMPLE # 3

The Ark of the Covenant also tells the story of redemption symbolically. Inside the Ark was the law of God, the Ten Commandments. 1 John 3:4 says, "Sin is the transgression of the law." The law (that which reveals man's sin) was covered by the Mercy Seat. The Mercy Seat was to be sprinkled with blood. This is a complete picture of redemption. Law (the Ten Commandments) and grace (the Mercy Seat) were reconciled by the blood sacrifice of Jesus Christ.

According to prophecy scholars, there are more than 2,500 prophecies in the Bible. To list them all is beyond the scope of this book. For those interested, *The Encyclopedia of Biblical Prophecy* by J. Barton Payne is an exhaustive record of every prophecy from Genesis to Revelation. So, we will confine ourselves to just a few of the more outstanding prophecies concerning Jesus Christ. Scholars point to over 300 specific prophecies that could in no way have been "self-fulfilled." The following eight prophecies should be enough to satisfy any honest sceptic.

MESSIANIC PROPHECY #1:
The Savior Is A Man Born Of The Seed Of A Woman

> And I will put enmity between you and the woman, and between your seed and her Seed; He shall bruise your head, and you shall bruise His heel (Gen. 3:15).

This is a record of what God said to Adam and Eve after the fall. A male child will be born of "the seed of a woman." In every other instance, when speaking of one's offspring, the Bible uses the term "the seed of the man." This prophecy eliminates 50% of all the people ever born—the Messiah will be a man. This also eliminates angels since they are not born of women. Whoever the Savior is, His birth will be unlike any other before or since, because women do not have "seed."

New Testament Fulfillment Of Prophecy #1

Now all this took place that what was spoken by the Lord through the prophet might be fulfilled, saying, "Behold, the virgin shall be with child, and shall bear a Son, and they shall call His name Immanuel," which translated means, "God with us" (Matt. 1:22-23).

MESSIANIC PROPHECY #2:
The Messiah Would Be A Descendant Of Abraham

Now the LORD had said to Abram: "Get out of your country, from your family and from your father's house, to a land that I will show you. I will make you a great nation; I will bless you and make your name great; and you shall be a blessing. I will bless those who bless you, and I will curse him who curses you; and in you all the families of the earth shall be blessed." (Gen. 12:1)

In this prophecy, one of Abraham's descendants is to be a blessing to *all the families of the earth*. How can one man bless all the families past, present and future? Jesus Christ redeemed the world from sin!

The New Testament Fulfillment Of Prophecy #2

This is the book of the genealogy of Jesus Christ, the son of David, the son of Abraham. (Matt. 1:1)

The very first verse in the New Testament (Matt. 1:1) shows us two things: first, that God always keeps His promises, and second, that the Bible is one book. This verse also shows that the Messiah had to have already come. Anyone claiming to be the Messiah had to be able to prove he was a direct descendant of David. The birth records were kept in the Temple. The Temple was destroyed in A.D. 70. When Christ returns, He won't need a birth certificate. Jesus is going to be revealed from Heaven with His mighty angels in flaming fire (2 Thess. 1:7-8)!

MESSIANIC PROPHECY #3:
The Messiah's Tribe

Judah, you are he whom your brothers shall praise; your hand shall be on the neck of your enemies; your father's children shall bow down before you. Judah is a lion's whelp; from the prey, my son, you have gone up. He bows down; he lies down as a lion; and as a lion, who shall rouse him? The scepter shall not depart from Judah, nor a lawgiver from between his feet, until Shiloh comes; and to Him shall be the obedience of the people (Gen. 49:8-10).

The New Testament Fulfillment Of Prophecy #3

For it is evident that our Lord was descended from Judah (Heb. 7:14, also see Rev. 5:5).

Here God eliminates eleven of the twelve tribes of Israel, and reveals that the Promised One will come from the tribe of Judah. The list of potential candidates to fulfill these prophecies grows smaller and smaller—by design.

MESSIANIC PROPHECY #4:
The Messiah's Family

Behold, the days are coming," declares the LORD, "When I shall raise up for David a righteous Branch; and He will reign as king and act wisely and do justice and righteousness in the land. "In His days Judah will be saved, and Israel will dwell securely; and this is His name by which He will be called, 'The LORD our righteousness'" (Jer. 23:5-6).

For a child will be born to us, a son will be given to us; and the government will rest on His shoulders; and His name will be called Wonderful Counselor, Mighty God, Eternal Father, Prince of Peace. There will be no end to the increase of {His} government or of peace, on the throne of David and over his kingdom, to establish it and to uphold it with justice and righteousness from then on and forevermore. The zeal of the LORD of hosts will accomplish this (Isa. 9:6).

Here, God eliminates all the families of the earth and says, that the Messiah will come from the family of David, making "Son of David" a Messianic title.

The New Testament Fulfillment Of Prophecy #4

. . . the angel Gabriel said to [Mary] "He will be great, and will be called the Son of the Most High; and the Lord God will give Him the throne of His father David" (Luke 1:26-32).

MESSIANIC PROPHECY #5:
The Place Of His Birth

But you, Bethlehem Ephrathah, though you are little among the thousands of Judah, yet out of you shall come forth to Me the One to be Ruler in Israel, whose goings forth are from of old, from everlasting (Micah 5:2).

Micah was written 700 years before Jesus was born. Here God eliminates all the other cities of the world and says the Messiah will be born in Bethlehem. Whoever this person is, He is from eternity past, He has no beginning and no end since his "goings forth are from of old, from everlasting." How significant is this prophecy? Imagine predicting where the President of the United Sates would be born 700 years in advance and getting it right!

The New Testament Fulfillment Of Prophecy #5

Now after Jesus was born in Bethlehem of Judea in the days of Herod the king, behold, magi from the east arrived in Jerusalem, saying, "Where is He who has been born King of the Jews? For we saw His star in the east, and have come to worship Him" (Matt. 2:1-2).

MESSIANIC PROPHECY #6:
His Miraculous Birth

Therefore the Lord Himself will give you a sign: behold, a virgin will be with child and bear a son, and she will call His name Immanuel (Isa. 7:14).

The New Testament Fulfillment Of Prophecy #6

But when he had considered this, behold, an angel of the Lord appeared to him in a dream, saying, "Joseph, son of David, do not be afraid to take Mary as your wife; for that which has been conceived in her is of the Holy Spirit. And she will bear a Son; and you shall call His name Jesus, for it is He who will save His people from their sins." Now all this took place that what was spoken by the Lord through the prophet might be fulfilled, saying, Behold, the virgin shall be with child, and shall bear a Son, and they shall call His name Immanuel," which translated means, "God with us" (Matt. 1:20).

The word translated "name" actually means title. Immanuel is a title meaning "God is with us." This literary device is used numerous times in Scripture when referring to Christ. Rev. 19:16 is another example...

And on His robe and on His thigh He has a name written, "KING OF KINGS, AND LORD OF LORDS."

MESSIANIC PROPHECY #7:
Isaiah prophesies that the servant of god would suffer, be beaten beyond recognition, be rejected by his own people, be silent before his accusers, die for our sin, and be buried in a borrowed tomb. He would be a man of peace.

He is despised and rejected by men, a Man of sorrows and acquainted with grief. And we hid, as it were, our faces from Him; he was despised, and we did not esteem Him.

Surely He has borne our griefs and carried our sorrows; yet we esteemed Him stricken, smitten by God, and afflicted. But He was wounded for our transgressions, he was bruised for our iniquities; the chastisement for our peace was upon Him, and by His stripes we are healed. All we like sheep have gone astray; we have turned, every one, to his own way; and the LORD has laid on Him the iniquity of us all. He was oppressed and He was afflicted, yet He opened not His mouth; He was led as a lamb to the slaughter, and as a sheep before its shearers is silent, so He opened not His mouth. He was taken from prison and from judgment, and who will declare His generation? For He was cut off from the land of the living; for the transgressions of My people He was stricken. And they made His grave with the wicked—but with the rich at His death, because He had done no violence, nor was any deceit in His mouth (Isa. 53:3).

The New Testament Fulfillment Of Prophecy #7

And when evening had come, they brought to Him many who were demon-possessed; and He cast out the spirits with a word, and healed all who were ill in order that what was spoken through Isaiah the prophet might be fulfilled, saying, "He Himself took our infirmities, and carried away our diseases" (Matt. 8:16-17).

MESSIANIC PROPHECY #8 :
Miracles Would Vindicate His Ministry

Isa. 42:6-9: "I am the LORD, I have called you in righteousness, I will also hold you by the hand and watch over you, and I will appoint you as a covenant to the people, as a light to the nations, To open blind eyes, to bring out prisoners from the dungeon, and those who dwell in darkness from the prison. I am the LORD, that is My name; I will not give My glory to another, nor My praise to graven images. Behold, the former things have come to pass, now I declare new things; before they spring forth I proclaim them to you."

The New Testament Fulfillment Of Prophecy #9

"Are You the Expected One, or shall we look for someone else?" And Jesus answered and said to them, "Go and report to John what you hear and see: the blind receive sight and the lame walk, the lepers are cleansed and the deaf hear, and the dead are raised up, and the poor have the gospel preached to them. And blessed is he who keeps from stumbling over Me" (Matt. 11:3-6).

SCIENCE SPEAKS ON PROPHECY

Peter Stoner, in his book *Science Speaks,* analyzed the chances of any one man fulfilling the Messianic prophecies by chance. For just eight prophecies to be fulfilled through one man is one chance in 100,000,000,000,000,000. The probability of 17 prophecies being fulfilled by one person is one chance in 480 followed by 30 zeros. The chance of 48 prophecies being fulfilled becomes a staggering—one chance in 10 with 157 zeros after it. This number is larger than the total number of atoms in the universe! There is only one man in all of history who fits the description of these prophecies. Jesus Christ alone fulfilled more than 300 specific ancient biblical prophecies.

According to PhD astrophysicist Hugh Ross, the odds of the more than 2,500 prophecies found in the Bible being fulfilled by chance are 1 with 200 zeros after it. According to the mathematical science of probability, if a number has more than 50 zeros after it, the possibility of that happening by chance is for all practical purposes, impossible.

THE MORAL ARGUMENT

This is the most powerful argument against all false religions. Why? Romans 2:15 says, God's moral law is written on every man's heart. The fact is, every man from the beginning of time until the end of the world, whether or not he has ever read a Bible or even heard of Jesus Christ, knows in his *heart* it's wrong to murder, it's wrong to steal, it's wrong to lie, it's wrong to have another man's wife, etc. As for those who reject the idea of absolute moral truth, Romans 1:18-20 is clear,

> For the wrath of God is revealed from heaven against all ungodliness and unrighteousness of men, who suppress the truth in unrighteousness, because that which is known about God is evident within them; for God made it evident to them.

> For since the creation of the world His invisible attributes, His eternal power and divine nature, have been clearly seen, being understood through what has been made, so that they are without excuse.

COMPARING THE TEN COMMANDMENTS IN THE BIBLE TO THE COMMANDMENTS OF MOHAMMED

Commandment #1:
You Shall Have No Other Gods Before Me

The English word translated LORD is YHWH in Hebrew. In the original Hebrew it literally means, I am the God who was, the God who is, and the God who always will be, the eternal, self-existent One. In Exodus 3:15, God said of Himself, "This is My name forever, and this is My memorial name to all generations."

More than 2000 years after God personally revealed His name [YHWH] to Moses, Mohammed is quoted in the Hadith as saying, "I have been commanded that I should fight these people till they bear witness that there is no god but Allah ... when they do this, their blood and their property shall be safe with me except as Islam requires."

Commandment #2:
You Are Not To Worship Or Bow Down
To Any Created Thing

The greatest act of worship in Islam is the required once-in-a-lifetime pilgrimage to Mecca. The high point is the ceremony at the religious shrine known as the Ka'aba. Muslims must run around the building counterclockwise seven times and, each time, pause to kiss a black rock that supposedly fell from heaven! Kissing a rock in a religious ceremony disobeys Commandment #2, not to worship any created thing.

Commandment #3:
Thou Shalt Not Take The Name Of The Lord In Vain

Will Durant in his classic, *The Story of Civilization*, writes, "Within the Ka'aba, in pre-Moslem days, were several idols representing gods. One was called Allah; three others were Allah's daughters, Al-Uzza, Al-Lat, and Al-Manat. We may judge the antiquity of this Arab pantheon from the mention of At-il-Lat (At-Lat) by Herodotus [fifth century B.C. Greek historian] as a major Arabian deity. The Quraish (Mohammed's tribe) paved the way for monotheism by worshiping Allah as chief god. Archaeological evidence uncovered in Arabia is overwhelming in demonstrating that the dominant pre-Islamic religion was the worship of the moon-god, Allah. Mohammed simply eliminated the other 359 deities, including Allah's daughters referred to in Sura 53:19!" (Cited by T.A. McMahon, *Berean Call*)

That is why you see the crescent moon on the Islamic flag and above Islamic temples. The God of the Bible is not the "moon god," He is the Creator of the moon. To address an idol as God is to disobey Commandments 1, 2, and 3!

Commandment #4:
Remember The Sabbath To Keep It Holy

Originally on Saturday, the Sabbath was changed to Sunday in order to commemorate the resurrection of Jesus Christ. Muslims worship on Friday.

Commandment #5:
Honor Your Father And Mother

While the main point of the fifth commandment is giving honor to whom honor is due, implied in this command is the idea that women are to be honored and are of equal value to men in the sight of God!

The Koran says (in Sura 4:38): "Men are superior to women," and gives men permission to "Remove them unto their beds, and beat them...." And they do!

The Bible says (in I Peter 3:7): "You husbands likewise, live with your wives in an understanding way, as with a weaker vessel, since she is a woman; and grant her honor as a fellow heir of the grace of life, so that your prayers may not be hindered."

In Eph. 5:28-29 the Bible also says, "So husbands ought also to love their own wives as their own bodies. He who loves his own wife loves himself, for no one ever hated his own flesh, but nourishes and cherishes it, just as Christ also does the church!" Following the Koran, regarding the physical abuse of women, disobeys Commandment #5. As a general rule, in most Islamic countries, women are treated as slaves.

Commandment #6:
Thou Shalt Not Murder

There are 123 verses in the Koran that call for fighting and killing anyone who does not believe this statement, "There is no God but Allah and Mohammed is his prophet." Jews and Christians are specifically named and targeted as such "infidels."

Sura 5:33 says, "...they [the infidels] shall be slain or crucified, or have their hands and feet cut off." In 9:5 it says, "Wage war against the infidels, as are your neighbors..." and in 47:3-9 a Muslim who cuts off the head of an "unbeliever" is promised paradise!

In John 16:2 Jesus prophesied...."an hour is coming for everyone who kills you to think that he is offering service to God."

In John 8:44 Jesus said, "You are of your father the devil, and you want to do the desires of your father. He was a murderer from the beginning, and does not stand in the truth, because there is no truth in him. Whenever he speaks a lie, he speaks from his own nature; for he is a liar, and the father of lies." And, in I Corinthians 6:9 the Bible says, "Murderers shall not inherit the kingdom of God."

Commandment #7:
Thou Shalt Not Commit Adultery

In Sura 4:2 the Koran says: "...of other women who seem good in your eyes, marry two, or three, or four; and if ye still fear that ye shall not act equitably, then one only; or the slaves you have acquired."

In 1 Cor. 6:9-10, the Bible says fornicators, and adulterers, shall not inherit the kingdom of God. But, the Koran endorses polygamy. In Islam a man can divorce his wife by repeating the phrase "I divorce you," three times. He is then free to marry again and again.

Nature itself proves that the doctrine of polygamy cannot be divinely inspired since the ratio of men to women has always been 50/50. If there were four (or more) women to every man in the world, this doctrine might not be so obviously false. In Matthew 19:5 Jesus said, "......a man shall leave his father and mother, and shall cleave to his wife; and the two shall become one flesh." Anything else is adultery.

The Koran goes on to say that the owner of any female slave can sell her into prostitution or rape her anytime he wants to, and Allah will forgive him! Don't believe it? Read it yourself in Sura 24:33:

Force not your female slave into sin. In order that you may enrich yourselves in this world, if they wish to preserve their modesty. Yet if any of you do compel them, afterward, God will forgive you.

Commandment #8:
Thou Shalt Not Steal

In Sura 24:29 the Koran says, "There shall be no harm in your entering houses in which no one dwells, for the supply of your needs." In other words, as long as no one is home, go in and take whatever you need! How would you feel if it was your house? In I Corinthians 6:9 the Bible says, ". . . thieves (*those who do not repent*) shall not inherit the kingdom of God."

Commandment #9:
Thou Shalt Not Lie

In Sura 5:91 the Koran says, "God will not punish you for a mistake in your oaths, but he will punish you for an oath taken seriously." The word "oath" means a solemn appeal to God for the truth of what is affirmed. In Matthew 5, Jesus said, "But I say to you, make no oath at all, . . . let your yes be yes and your no be no; anything beyond this is of evil."

In Rev. 21 the Bible says, "All liars will have their place in the lake of fire and brimstone which is the second death." Islam actually has a doctrine known as Taqiyya (pronounced tark-e-ya) which calls for the use of deception and lies to expedite its growth and advance its agenda. It is synonymous with Kitman, which means to conceal their malevolent intentions. Taqiyya and Kitman are also known as "holy hypocrisy".

In John 8:44 Jesus reveals the source of lying,

> You are of your father the devil, and the desires of your father you want to do. He was a murderer from the beginning, and does not stand in the truth, because there is no truth in him. When he speaks a lie, he speaks from his own resources, for he is a liar and the father of it.

Jesus' strongest words of condemnation were reserved for religious hypocrites in Matthew chapter 23. In Revelation chapter 21 God's Word says, "All liars will have their place in the lake of fire and brimstone which is the second death."

Commandment #10:
Thou Shalt Not Covet

To covet is to enviously desire something that belongs to someone else. That is what wars come from. Covetousness is idolatry according to Col. 3. Inside of covetousness is lust, greed, and pride. No one is free from committing this sin at one time or another.

CONCLUSION:

Not everyone who says to Me, "Lord, Lord," will enter the kingdom of heaven; but he who does the will of My Father who is in heaven. Many will say to Me on that day, "Lord, Lord, did we not prophesy in Your name, and in Your name cast out demons, and in Your name perform many miracles?" And then I will declare to them, "I never knew you; depart from Me, you who practice lawlessness." Matt. 7:21-23

CHAPTER FOUR

QUESTIONS ABOUT THE KORAN AND THE HADITH

ASK...

- *Are there any scientific statements in the Koran that are false?*

  In Sura 18:86 the Koran says: "When he reached the setting of the sun, he found that it set in a pond of murky water."

- *Do you believe that the sun sets in a puddle of mud?*

- *The Hadith says that Adam was 60 cubits tall; that is 90 feet or nine stories high Do you really believe that?*

  The Hadith Bukhari vol. IV, no. 543: "The Prophet said, 'Allah created Adam, making him 60 cubits tall.'"

ASK...

- *Is it true that non-Muslims have seven intestines, and Muslims only have one?*

  Ibn Umar reported Allah's Messenger as saying: "A non-Muslim eats in seven intestines while a Muslim eats in one intestine." (See also nos. 5114-5120, The Hadith Muslim vol. III, no. 5113, chapter 862).

  Neither science, nor *The Guinness Book of World Records* has ever reported discovering a man with seven intestines.

- *Do you believe this statement by Mohammed is correct?*

ASK...

- *In light of what we know about human genes, how do you account for the answer to third question below?*

    The Hadith Bukhari vol. IV. no 546: "When Abdullah bin Salam heard of the arrival of the Prophet at Medina, he came to him and said, 'I am going to ASK... you about three things which nobody knows except a prophet:

1. What is the first sign of the Hour (i.e. the end of the world)?

    Allah's prophet said, "Gabriel just now told me of their answers." Abdullah said, "He (i.e. Gabriel), from amongst all the angels, is the enemy of the Jews." Allah's Apostle said, "The first sign of the Hour will be a fire that will bring together the people from the East to the West."

2. What will be the first meal taken by the people of Paradise?

    "The first meal of the people of Paradise will be an extra lobe of fish-liver."

3. Why does a child resemble its father, and why does it resemble its maternal uncle?"

    "As for the resemblance of the child to its parents: If a man has sexual intercourse with his wife and gets his discharge first, the child will resemble the father, and if the woman gets her discharge first, the child will resemble her."

- *Based on these answers, was Mohammed a prophet?*

- *In Sura 23:14, the Koran says that man was formed from a clot of blood, and in other places it says we were formed from dust. Which is true?*

- *Mohammed said, if a Muslim looks up to the sky while crying out in prayer to Allah, his eyes will be snatched away.*

Abu Huraira reported Allah's Apostle saying: "People should avoid lifting their eyes towards the sky while supplicating in prayer, otherwise their eyes would be snatched away."

ASK...

- *Is that true or not? If it is not true, then what is it?*

ASK...

- *Do flies have a disease on one wing and the cure for that disease on the other?*

  The Hadith Bukhari vol. IV, no. 537: Narrated Abu Huraira: The Prophet said, "If a house fly falls into the drink of anyone of you, he should dip it (into the drink) because one of its wings has a disease and the other wing has the cure."

- *Can you explain exactly how the night, the day, the sun, the moon, and the stars are subject unto you?*

  Sura 16:12 says: "And He hath subjected to you the night and the day; the sun and the moon and the stars too are subjected to you by his behest.

  Muslims often claim that the greatest proof that the Koran is divinely inspired is based on the eloquence of its literature—that in its original language it is perfect and unsurpassed in eloquence.

ASK...

- *Do you read Arabic?*

- *Did you know that among Arabic scholars it is common knowledge that the Koran is filled with errors in grammar and sentence structure, and much of what is written it is incoherent?*

- *If you doubt that the Koran is subject to error, consider the following quote from a Muslim scholar commenting on the obvious grammatical mistakes in the Koran:*

  "The Qur'an contains sentences which are incomplete and not fully intelligible without the aid of commentaries; foreign words, unfamiliar Arabic words, and words used with other than the normal meaning; adjectives and verbs inflected without observance of the concords of gender and number; illogically and ungrammatically applied pronouns which sometimes have no referent; and predicates which in rhymed passages are often remote from the subjects... To sum up, more than one hundred Qur'anic aberrations from the normal rules and structure of Arabic have been noted." (Dashti, 23 Years, pgs.48-50)

- *If Allah really is the author of the Koran, shouldn't we expect the original Arabic grammar to be perfect?*

ASK...

- *If Islam is true, why does the Koran forbid Muslims from examining the evidence?*

  Sura 5:101: "ASK... not questions about things which, if made plain to you may cause you trouble.... Some people before you did ASK... such questions, and on account lost their faith in Islam."

- *Why do you suppose these people, to whom Mohammed referred, lost their faith after examining the evidence?*

  Compare that to the Bible's teaching in Acts 17:11. "There the Bereans were *commended* by the Apostles for searching the Scriptures to find out if what they (the Apostles) were teaching was correct!"

- *In Sura 17:90-95 the Koran clearly says Mohammed performed no miracles, but the Hadith says he did. Here is one example:*

  The Hadith Burkhari vol. I, no. 170: "He put his hand in that pot and ordered the people to perform ablution from it. I saw the water springing out from underneath his fingers."

- *Islam teaches that both books have equal authority. Which one is wrong?*

ASK...

- *Doesn't Islam condemn hypocrisy?*

  Sura 2:256 says, "Let there be no compulsion in religion."

ASK...

- *Jihad calls for the death of all who refuse to accept the teachings of Mohammed, whether they believe it or not. How is that not "compulsion in religion?" How do you explain this obvious contradiction?*

CHAPTER FIVE

QUESTIONS ABOUT MOHAMMED

ASK...

- *The Hadith says that Mohammed had marital relations with a nine-year-old girl. This example has been repeated by many Muslim men. Is this an example of Islamic virtue?*

The Hadith Burkhari vol. V, no. 234: Narrated Aisha: "The Prophet was engaged to me when I was a girl six years old . . . I was playing in a swing with some of my girl-friends . . . Unexpectedly Allah's Apostle came to me in the afternoon and my mother handed me over to him. At that time I was a girl of nine years of age."

Burkhari vol. V, no. 236: "The Prophet . . . married Aisha when she was a girl of six years of age and consummated the marriage when she was nine years old."

Compare that to what Jesus said about children:

Luke 17:2 "It would be better for him if a millstone were hung around his neck, and he were thrown into the sea, than that he should offend one of these little ones."

ASK...

- *Sura 4:3 says a man may have four wives. How can Islam claim that Mohammed was the greatest example of virtue when he had at least eleven?*

- *Is Mohammed contradicting his own teaching or not?*

ASK...

- *Mohammed said, Satan urinates in the ear of a Muslim who fails to pray. How can Satan urinate, since he is a non-material being?*

- *Since Satan is not omnipresent, with more than one billion Muslims in the world, how does he enforce this rule?*

> The Hadith Burkhari vol. II, no. 245: "If one sleeps and does not offer the prayer, Satan urinates in his ears. Narrated Abdullah: The Prophet said, 'Satan urinated in his ears.'"

- *Mohammed said that Satan will spend the night in your nose if you become ceremonially unclean. Wouldn't Satan have to be omniscient, and omnipresent to enforce this rule?*

> The Hadith Bukhari vol. IV, no. 516: "Satan stays in the upper part of the nose all night."

> Muslim vol. I, no. 462: "The Apostle of Allah said, "When any one of you awakes from sleep and performs ablution, he must clean his nose three times, for the devil spends the night in the interior of his nose."

ASK...

- *What would you think if you saw a man fall to the ground, holding the sides of his head trying to stop the ringing in his ears because it is so loud, his face is turned red, he is shaking violently, his eyes are open wide, his lips are trembling, saliva is dripping from his mouth, he is sweating profusely, snorting like an animal, and so afraid when it was over he would hide under a blanket?*

> According to the Hadith, that this is how Mohammed would react when he would receive his revelations from the "angel of light" who called himself Gabriel. *(Vol. I,*

nos. 2, 3, 4; vol. II, chap. 16 (pg. 354), 544; vol. III, nos. 17, 829; vol. IV, nos. 95, 438, 458, 461; vol. V, nos. 170, 462, 18, 659; vol. VI, nos. 447, 448, 468, 478, 481.)

ASK….

• **Does this description sound like a man who may be either insane or demon possessed?**

Mohammed said he received his revelations from an "Angel of light." Did you know that 600 years before Mohammed was born, 2 Corinthians 11:14 said that Satan can transform himself into an angel of light?

ASK…

• **The Bible says that magic arts and sorcery are from Satan. Were you aware that the Hadith says that Mohammed was under a magic spell?**

The Hadith Burkhari vol. VII. no. 658: Narrated Aisha: "A man called Labid bin al-A'samrom the tribe of Bani Zaraiq worked magic on Allah's Apostle until Allah's Apostle started imagining that he had done a thing that he had not really done."

Burkhari vol. VII, no. 660: Narrated Aisha: "Magic was worked on Allah's Apostle so that he used to think that he had had sexual relations with his wives while he actually had not . . . "He is under the effect of magic."

Burkhari vol, VII, no. 661: Narrated Aisha: "Magic was worked on Allah's Apostle so that he began to imagine that he had done something although he had not."

ASK…

• **What is the test of a true prophet? Deuteronomy 18:20-22 says there is one test of a true prophet, by if what he prophecies** *comes true 100% of the time. One false prophecy incurred the death sentence.*

ASK...

- *Do you know what the Koran says about how you can know that Mohammed was a prophet?*

  Jabir B. Samura reported: "I saw the Seal on his back as if it were a pigeon's egg."

  Abdullah b. Sarjis reported: "I saw Allah's Apostle and ate with him bread and meat... I then went after him and saw the Seal of Prophethood between his shoulders on the left side of this shoulder having spots like moles."

ASK...

- *How does Mohammed's mole qualify him as a prophet?*

ASK...

- *Would a true prophet know the difference between the hour of God's judgment and a solar eclipse?*

  The Hadith Burkhari vol. 11, no. 167: "The sun eclipsed and the Prophet jumped up terrified that it might be the Hour of Judgment."

- *How can Mohammed promise eternal life to Muslims who "martyr" themselves, when speaking of the afterlife, since he had no assurance of salvation himself?*

  The Hadith Burkhari vol. V, no. 266: "The Prophet said, "By Allah, even though I am the Apostle of Allah, yet I do not know what Allah will do to me."

ASK...

- *Mohammed taught that men are superior to women, and have the right to beat their wives.*

  Sura 4:34: "Men are the managers of the affairs of women... those you fear may be rebellious, admonish; banish them to their couches, and beat them."

- *Compare that to the Bible's teaching:*

  1 Pet. 3:7: "Husbands, likewise, dwell with them with understanding, giving honor to the wife, as to the weaker vessel, and as being heirs together of the grace of life, that your prayers may not be hindered."

  Eph. 5:28-29: "So husbands ought to love their own wives as their own bodies; he who loves his wife loves himself. For no one ever hated his own flesh, but nourishes and cherishes it, just as the Lord does the church."

- *In virtually every country in the world statistics show that men are far more immoral than women, and the vast majority of crime is committed by men. Why is it then, that Mohammed said women are more immoral, less intelligent, and more ungrateful than men are?*

  The Hadith Burkhari vol. I, no. 28: "The Prophet said, "I was shown the Hell-fire and that the majority of its dwellers were women who were ungrateful."

  Burkhari vol. I, no. 301: Allah's Apostle said, "O women! Give alms, as I have seen that the majority of the dwellers of Hell-fire were you women... I have not seen anyone more deficient in intelligence and religion than you."

  Burkhari vol. II, no. 161: The Prophet then said…"I also saw the Hell-fire and I had never seen such a horrible sight. I saw that most of the inhabitants were women."

ASK...

- *Would you mind asking a Muslim wife which one of the above she considers to be divinely inspired?*

- *According to Mohammad, if a Muslim passes gas while he is praying, his prayer is unacceptable until he performs ablution. Why would that be?*

  Vol. 1, Book 4, no.137. Allah's Apostle said, "The prayer of a person who does Hadith (passes urine, stool or wind) is not accepted till he performs (repeats) the ablution." A person from Hadaramout asked Abu Huraira, "What is 'Hadith?'" Abu Huraira replied, 'Hadith' means the passing of wind from the anus."

- *If passing gas in prayer is unclean, why would Mohammed order people to drink the urine of a Camel?*

  The Hadith Burkhari vol. I, no. 234: "The Prophet ordered them to go to the herd of camels and to drink their milk and urine."

- *If a man is in hell, how could putting palm leaves on his grave relieve his suffering?*

  The Hadith Burkhari vol. II, no. 443: "The Prophet passed by two graves and those persons (in the graves) were being tortured... He then took a green leaf of a date-palm tree, split it into two pieces and fixed one on a grave."

  The people said, "O Allah's Apostle! Why have you done so?" He replied, "I hope that their punishment be lessened until they (i.e. the palm leaves) become dry."

ASK...

- *Do you believe a man has ever been changed into a rat?*

  Bukhari, vol. IV, no. 524, pg. 333: The Prophet said, "A group of Israelites were lost. Nobody knows what they did. But I do not see them except that they were cursed and transformed into rats, for if you put the milk of a she-camel in front of a rat, it will not drink it, but if the milk of a sheep is put in front of it, it will drink it."

- *The Bible says: "A righteous man is kind to his beast." If a man is cruel to animals, what does that make him?*

  The Hadith Bukhari vol. IV, nos. 539: The Prophet said, "Angels do not enter a house which has either a dog or a picture in it."

  Muslim vol. III, no. 3810: Ibn Umar reported: Allah's Messenger ordered us to kill dogs and he sent men to the corners of Medina that they should be killed.

  Muslim vol. III, no. 3813: Allah's Messenger ordered us to kill dogs and we carried out this order so much that we also killed the dog coming with a woman from the desert.... He said, "It is your duty to kill the jet black dog having two spots, for it is the devil."

ASK...

- *Did you know that playing chess is unclean according to Mohammed?*

  The Hadith Muslim vol. IV, no. 5612 Chapter 946: Allah's Apostle said, "He who played chess is like one who dyed his hand with the flesh and blood of swine."

ASK...

- *Are you willing to risk your eternal destiny on a religion that teaches that if you disagree with any of these doctrines you must die as an infidel and burn in hell?*

CHAPTER SIX

THE TRI-UNITY OF GOD

In order to understand Islam, you need to know that from childhood, Muslim children are taught the doctrines of tawhid and shirk. These are two of the most essential doctrines in Islam. Tawhid is the strictest form of unitarian monotheism. It is the absolute oneness of god. Tawhid is an absolute commandment in Islam. Tawhid is the greatest commandment and Shirk the greatest sin.

Shirk is the sin of polytheism. It refers to serving anything other than Allah. Muslims are taught that Shirk is worse than murder, rape, child abuse, or incest. They are taught that believing doctrines such as the deity of Christ and the Trinity are the most heinous of all crimes.

Christ's teaching on the Trinity, the incarnation, and His atoning death on the cross are dogmatically labeled as "gross blasphemies" in Islam. Muslim children are told that Christians are pagan idol- worshippers. Many have been told that the doctrine of Christ dying on the cross for our sin is as archaic and pagan as a human sacrifice to some "volcano god." We are accused of believing in a God who is a child-abuser, and the God of the Bible has been called a "blood- thirsty vampire." That is about as far away from John 3:16 as you can get!

In order to help the Muslim understand that the Trinity is not unreasonable or unfathomable, you can demonstrate the principle of the Trinity so even a child can understand it. The fact is God created tri-unities all around us. Scientists tell us that the universe consists of three things: Time, space, and matter; a trinity of trinities.

Time: the past, the present, and the future. The past is not the present, the present is not the future, and the future is not the past. "One is not the other, all are part of the same, none can exist without the other, and yet each is distinct" (A. Rogers).

Space: We live in a three dimensional world: Height, width, and depth. Height is not width, width is not depth, and depth is not height. One is not the other, all are part of the same, none can exist without the other, and yet each is distinct.

Matter: All matter is made up of atoms. Atoms have three main elements: protons, neutrons and electrons. Protons are not neutrons, neutrons are not electrons, electrons are not protons. One is not the other, all are part of the same, no atom can exist without the other, and yet each one is distinct.

Man: According to I Thes. 5:23, man (made in the image of God) has a triune nature: spirit, soul, and body. Have you ever justified doing something in your mind, and after doing it, your heart, beating faster than normal, said, "You shouldn't have done that?" That is your spirit speaking to your soul! One is not the other, all are part of the same, none can exist without the other, and yet each is distinct

The human mind: The mind consists of the mind (intellect) the will and the emotions. Your mind is not your will, the will is not the emotions, and the emotions are not the mind. One is not the other, all are part of the same, none can exist without the other, and yet each one is distinct!

There is not a scientist on earth who can tell you how a brown cow can eat green grass and turn it into white milk! The point is, whether or not you can rationally understand something does not preclude you from believing it!

There is no logical reason whatsoever that Almighty God cannot sit on the throne in heaven, come to earth as a man, and fill the universe with His Spirit all at the same time. How can a man (who has never seen God) say God cannot? The Bible says, "Nothing is impossible with God."

REMEMBER WHAT GOD ASKED JOB?

Job 38:4: "Where were you when I laid the foundations of the earth? Tell Me, if you have understanding."

THE FATHERHOOD OF GOD

A well-known seminary in the United States interviewed 600 former Muslims who converted to Christianity. One common thread that ran through each of their testimonies was how attracted they were to the biblical concept of the fatherhood of God. The idea that one can know God and have a personal, intimate relationship with Him is nowhere to be found in Islam!

Christianity is not a religion, it is a revelation. That revelation leads to a personal relationship with God our Father through Jesus Christ. This truth is very compelling to Muslims since "Allah" is unknowable. Here are some verses you can use to show Muslims what God's Word says about our relationship to Him.

Exod. 20:1-3: And God spoke all these words, saying: "I am the LORD *your* God, who brought you out of the land of Egypt, out of the house of bondage. You shall have no other gods before Me."

Deut. 4:29: "But from there you will seek the LORD your God, and you will find Him if you seek Him with all your heart and with all your soul."

2 Chr. 7:14: "If my people, who are called by my name, will humble themselves and pray and seek My face and turn from their wicked ways, then will I hear from heaven and will forgive their sin and will heal their land."

Jer. 24:7: "Then I will give them a heart to know Me, that I am the LORD; and they shall be My people, and I will be their God, for they shall return to Me with their whole heart."

Prov. 2:1-5: "My son, if you receive my words, and treasure my commands within you, So that you incline your ear to wisdom, and apply your heart to understanding; Yes, if you cry out for discernment, and lift up your voice for understanding, If you seek her as silver, and search for her as for hidden treasures; Then you will understand the fear of the LORD, and find the knowledge of God."

Matt. 7:7-8: "Ask and it shall be given you; seek, and you shall find; knock, and it shall be opened unto you: For every one that ASK...s receives; and he that seeks finds; and to him who knocks it shall be opened."

John 3:16: "For God so loved the world that He gave His only begotten Son, that whoever believes in Him should not perish but have everlasting life."

John 17:3: "And this is eternal life, that they may know You, the only true God, and Jesus Christ whom You have sent."

Rom. 8:15-16: "For you did not receive the spirit of bondage again to fear, but you received the Spirit of adoption by whom we cry out, 'Abba, Father.' The Spirit Himself bears witness with our spirit that we are children of God."

2 Cor. 6:16-18: "And what agreement has the temple of God with idols? For you are the temple of the living God. As God has said: "I will dwell in them and walk among them. I will be their God, and they shall be My people." Therefore "Come out from among them and be separate, says the Lord. Do not touch what is unclean, and I will receive you." "I will be a Father to you, and you shall be My sons and daughters, says the Lord Almighty."

Gal. 4:6-7: "And because you are sons, God has sent forth the Spirit of His Son into your hearts, crying out, "Abba, Father!" Therefore you are no longer a slave but a son, and if a son, then an heir of God through Christ."

James 4:7-8: "Submit therefore to God. Resist the devil and he will flee from you. Draw near to God and He will draw near to you. Cleanse your hands, you sinners; and purify your hearts, you double-minded."

I Jn. 5:13: "These things I have written to you who believe in the name of the Son of God, that you may know that you have eternal life, and that you may continue to believe in the name of the Son of God."

I Jn. 1:1-4: "That which was from the beginning, which we have heard, which we have seen with our eyes, which we have looked upon, and our hands have handled, concerning the Word of life-the life was manifested, and we have seen, and bear witness, and declare to you that eternal life which was with the Father and was manifested to us—that which we have seen and heard we declare to you, that you also may have fellowship with us; and truly our fellowship is with the Father and with His Son Jesus Christ. And these things we write to you that your joy may be full."

Rev. 3:20: "Behold, I stand at the door and knock. If anyone hears My voice and opens the door, I will come in to him and dine with him, and he with Me."

COMPARE THE WORDS OF JESUS

Buddha: "I am a teacher in search of truth."
Jesus: "I Am the truth."

Confucius: "I never claimed to be holy."
Jesus: "Which one of you convicts Me of sin?"

Mohammed: "I do not know what Allah will do to me."
Jesus: "I Am the resurrection and the life. He who believes in Me, though he die, yet shall he live."

None of these other men ever claimed to be God. They all said God is this way, go this way.

Jesus said: "*I Am the way, the truth and the life; no man comes to the Father but by Me*"!

APPENDIX ONE

COMPARING THE LITERATURE OF THE KORAN TO THE BIBLE

The Koran's opening verse:

Praise be to God, lord of the worlds.

The Bible's opening verse:

In the beginning God created the heavens and the earth.

In The Middle Of The Koran (Sura 34:3)

"He knoweth what entereth into the earth, and what proceedeth from it; and what cometh down from heaven, and what goeth up into it: and He is the Merciful, the Forgiving! 'Never,' say the unbelievers, 'will the Hour come upon us!' Say: Yea, by my Lord who knoweth the unseen, it will surely come upon you! not the weight of a mote either in the Heavens or in the Earth escapeth him; nor is there aught less than this or aught greater, which is not in the clear Book."

In The Middle Of The Bible (Ps. 23:1-6).

"The Lord is my shepherd; I shall not want. He makes me to lie down in green pastures; he leads me beside the still waters.

He restores my soul; he leads me in the paths of righteousness for His name's sake. Yea, though I walk through the valley of the shadow of death, I will fear no evil; for thou art with me; thy rod and thy staff, they comfort me. You prepare a table before me in the presence of my enemies; you anoint my head with oil; my cup runs over.

Surely goodness and mercy shall follow me all the days of my life; and I will dwell in the house of the LORD forever."

The Closing Verses Of The Koran

"In the Name of God, the Compassionate, the Merciful SAY: I betake me for refuge to the Lord of the DAYBREAK Against the mischiefs of his creation; And against the mischief of the night when it overtaketh me; And against the mischief of weird women; I And against the mischief of the envier when he envieth." "in the Name of God, the Compassionate, the Merciful Say: I betake me for refuge to the Lord of MEN, The King of men, The God of men, Against I the, mischief of the stealthily withdrawing whisperer, Who whispereth in man's breast Against djinn and men."

The Closing Verses Of The Bible

"I, Jesus, have sent My angel to testify to you these things for the churches. I am the root and the offspring of David, the bright morning star." And the Spirit and the bride say, "Come." And let the one who hears say, "Come." And let the one who is thirsty come; let the one who wishes take the water of life without cost.

I testify to everyone who hears the words of the prophecy of this book: if anyone adds to them, God shall add to him the plagues which are written in this book; and if anyone takes away from the words of the book of this prophecy, God shall take away his part from the tree of life and from the holy city, which are written in this book. He who testifies to these things says, "Yes, I am coming quickly." Amen. Come, Lord Jesus. The grace of the Lord Jesus be with all. Amen."